THIRD CHAPTER OF LIFE ADVENTURES

I0476192

A BABY BOOMERS GUIDE TO ENJOYING THE THIRD CHAPTER OF LIFE!

Eric C. Hughes and Debbie Finley

ISBN-13: 978-1512378412
ISBN-10: 1512378410

i

SPECIAL OPPORTUNITY!

When you have finished reading this book, please go to the last page and find out how YOU can become involved in the Third Chapter community.

We have created several resources where you can share your experiences, hopes, dreams and results with other Third Chapter travelers.

We have provided numerous contact resources for you throughout this book and the final page has some very special contact opportunities for you to make use of.

Here is to having a fantastic Third Chapter Adventure yourself!

Acknowledgements

Debbie and I would like to acknowledge and thank all of our family and friends that have supported us during the creation of this book. Because we have the equivalent of 4 basketball teams in our combined family of kids and grandkids, we can't name you all.....but you know who you are and we love you guys' lots.

I would want to thank Arsen Marsoobian for his inspiring book, *Don't Die*, and for encouraging me to continue this process. Thanks Papa Soob!

We would also like to thank and acknowledge our individual "parental units", without whom we would not even be here in the first place and who are wholly responsible for the initial sets of stepping stones that we had to tread upon.

Preface

What is the Third Chapter? How does it work? Can I be part of it? What do I do and how do I do it? And why do Baby Boomers have a special interest in this phase of life? The purpose in writing this book is to share with people what the Third Chapter concept is, how to embrace it and how to connect with other like-minded individuals who are on their own Third Chapter adventure.

Baby Boomers are defined as people born between 1946 and 1964 and the Boomer part refers to the explosion of births following the return home of all of the G.I.s after the end of WWII. So if you are one, you know it and feel it. Just a little age reference there. We were the test babies for a myriad of social, educational and economic experiments during this time and as we as a group are moving into this phase of our lives, we are setting the standard for how to successfully enjoy our Third Chapter adventure.

And I want to make sure everyone understands the terms we use throughout this book. When we refer to your journey, your trip or your adventure, we are not strictly speaking about actual travel. We are referring to the life journey, the trek that we are all on. For you, that journey may actually mean getting in a vehicle and driving. But basically we are referring to getting up and getting going on whatever life choice you make for this particular portion of your existence.

In other words, do you want to retire or write a new chapter in your life? A recent study shows that over 50% of people over 50 are moving into some type of entrepreneur lifestyle. That they are writing a new chapter. Couple this with the facts that this group is growing significantly as more and more Baby Boomers move into this section of their lives, have a longer life expectancy, have more disposable income and still want to lead meaningful and vibrant lives.

We hope that you will enjoy the book, share your own stories with us and help fellow travelers in their Third Chapter adventure live it as fully and as completely as possible. At the end of each chapter there will be a My Adventure Plan Page where we encourage you to start putting together your own adventure and begin mapping out how to identify, start and enjoy this wonderful chapter of your life. Additional resources to help you along the way are included throughout the book so enjoy, have a good time getting your journey worked out and have a blast as you navigate your way through YOUR Third Chapter Adventure.

Contents

What's Ahead?

So, Who am I and Where Am I?

"Twenty years from now you will be more disappointed by the things you didn't do than by the ones you did do. So throw off the bowlines. Sail away from the safe harbor. Catch the trade winds in your sails. Explore. Dream. Discover." — Mark Twain

The phrase Third Chapter Of Life started coming into vogue and general usage several years ago. It refers to that period in a person's life that fits, sometimes not to neatly, between getting to the end of one's work career and having to take up permanent residence in an assisted living facility. You know, that gray area sometimes referred to as RETIREMENT. Or in some cases, Preretirement.

As generally accepted by this concept, a person's first chapter is the learning period. We all go to elementary school, high school, college for a large number of us, possibly some military experience and we spend the first 18 to 25 years or so of our lives learning. We learn very critical things, like the Pythagorean Principle and all about acute and obtuse angles. And subjugating verbs, although why a verb would stand for being subjugated is beyond me. So unless you went into engineering or became an English major, you probably never, ever used any of these again. I know I sure didn't.

There has always been a normal progression to things. You are a kid with all the freedom that implies (except for school, of course). In our minds, school was invented to ruin a young person's free time. His goofing off time. Her carefree time. School was invented to be just plain mean. But hopefully somewhere in this period of imposed detention, we actually learned something. Even though I primarily learned how to goof off and get away with stupid stuff without being caught, sometimes things would happen in my adult life where I actually knew the answer, which indicates that at least some of this education stuck. I am not sure how because at the time I was diligently striving to make sure I learned NOTHING! And I am sure I am not the only one with this type of experience.

Then you graduate and go out into the real world. Awesome. I am going to set the world on fire. Do great things. Make a real mark for myself. And then reality hits. OMG! I actually have to work. No one else is going to pay for my house, food, car, music, meals, recreation, toys.....Man, and this stuff actually costs MONEY. And so ends our carefree (more or less) First Chapter.

The Second Chapter is that career, that adult life, that when you were 25 seemed so far off and distant but is now only a fond memory.

You had all these vivid and clear images in your mind of what you were going to do, how successful you were going to be and what a magnificent mark you were going to leave on the world. But now, you are nearing or at the end of this phase in your life and you have to look back and reflect on how you actually did. Kind of a life midterm exam. Did I get done all that I had started out to do? By my own gauge, did I do it right or did I miss the mark some of the time?

What grade would you give yourself? And, finally, how come I didn't have more time to do all the things I wanted to do?

Have you ever noticed that the older you get, the faster time flies by? When I was 11, sixth grade seemed to take 3.5 years to get over. Now, the last 3 years only seemed to take about 18 months to get through. Maybe I can apply for a federal grant to study this time space continuum issue. Hey, they pay good money to find out why frogs croak so why not for this?

You may be among the lucky few that were able to find a vocation that you not only loved but that also provided a great income. If you are in this group, then you have truly had a blessed Second Chapter that has allowed you to be involved in a profession or position that fed your passion and gave you a great sense of accomplishment and satisfaction.

Having had numerous discussions on this topic with fellow travelers, I believe that the majority of us worked in a profession or professions that were ok, that didn't drive us to drink or make us run down the street screaming but that were not totally fulfilling in every aspect. Whether you were doing something that was your life's passion or just marking time in a job that got you through, the end result is the same. We get to finally stop and smell the roses. Or plant the roses. Or pull rose thorns from our hands. Whatever. The point is we have now reached our Third Chapter.

So, now that you are here, what do you do? The conventional wisdom of our parents and grandparents is that now you retire and get to finally enjoy life. The problem is that mom never really shared how this was supposed to be done. One day you are finishing an 8 hour, normal work day and the very next day you have nothing to do. Zero. Zilch. Nada. But now you have all this time to enjoy your life, to take up space on a porch swing and wait for something to happen, to finally just savor your life. Sounds awesome. Also sounds like you have just suddenly shut down the act of actually living and are just waiting for space to open up at a local retirement home or facility where you can do crafts on Thursdays. Not really what I had in my game plan all those years ago when I started this adventure.

My friend Arsen Marsoobian gave me a great example of this. The first part of his Third Chapter was spent playing golf, a lot of golf, every day of every week for a couple of years. The he realized he was just marking time and not really doing anything. His observation was that the only difference between retirees on a golf course and a cemetery is that some of the bodies are above ground and some are below ground.

His point was that even though he was no longer fully actively involved in his normal work life, he really wasn't living. He was just marking time. (For a full account of his remarkable story, please check out his book "Don't Die" on Amazon. It is well worth the read)

And THIS is where your Third Chapter exists. As far as I am concerned, next to having had my kids and grandkids, this is the payoff. This is the reward that I have been struggling to reach for lo these many years. But what do I actually do now and how do I do it?

Through our talks and travels, I have come to believe that even the luckiest among us who have had a career that was perfect, that met all of their requirements and gave them a truly blessed life also harbor another desire or passion that they still have not satisfied. That there is still some inside itch that we haven't scratched yet that we need to satisfy and so we all have the same opportunity to experience an awesome Third Chapter journey in our own special ways.

Some folks that were business owners begin working in the arts; sculpting, painting, woodwork or whatever. Leaders in business and industry that have always had this little voice in the back of their minds telling them they needed to paint, to weld sculptures, to write that next great American novel. They discover that inner creativity that they had to suppress for so long. Some people find a new life in a second career in some field of endeavor they had always dreamed of but never had the opportunity to indulge themselves in. Like becoming a motivational speaker and passing their accumulated wisdom on to others. Or starting their own specialty business like an arts and crafts store, a yogurt stand, a unique restaurant or a tattoo parlor. Look, it's YOUR Third Chapter – who am I to judge?

The WHAT you can now participate in is entirely up to you. And there are no wrong answers here (you may see this thought a couple of more times in the coming pages) for you to worry about. If it is legal, ethical, satisfies your basal inner needs, feeds your passion and doesn't hurt anyone, then just go for it.

And then there are people like Debbie and I. Kind of like Third Chapter catchalls. We want to do creative things around the house, like really cool landscaping or chalk painting all the furniture to fall into the Shabby Chic / Distressed design style. Our watch word is Eclectic. Eclectic to the max.

We also want to travel, to explore new areas, to boldly go where no other Third Chapter-ite has gone before! Ok, so I watch too much Star Trek but you get the picture.

So we want to combine a lot of things. First we had to figure out exactly what those things were and then design a plan to make this work. Over a period of time, we got to the point that we could start exploring our Third Chapter adventures. We determined that we could in fact travel AND work at the same time. We discovered that all of our kids could, miraculously, survive on their own without us being constantly on deck to provide any assistance we just knew that they would need us for. And most importantly, we found out that we could seriously enjoy ourselves doing all this. Which I guess is pretty much the point of embracing your Third Chapter life anyway.

Shortly we will look at how to get going on your own journey with baby steps but for now, let me give you a brief explanation of how we got to the point that we are at so you can understand the point of view we are coming from.

We started very small. At the time, it just seemed that we were doing normal dating type activities but as we grew in our relationship and took a closer look at where we were headed, we realized that we were actually taking trial steps towards the ultimate Third Chapter experience we both really wanted to achieve.

We started with day trips into the Sequoias and surrounding area and then moved into two and three day trips to the coast and metropolitan areas in California. What these trips allowed us to do was to have some great conversations about what we were doing, how these explorations felt to us and where we ultimately wanted to get to at this point in each of our lives.

The upshot of all of this was that we both agreed and understood that instead of working as long and hard as we could and then immediately going into a formal, possible very short lived, retirement mode, that what we actually wanted to do was keep working only as long as we had to and then develop a strategy to fully embrace our Third Chapter and live life as fully and completely as we could. You see there is a huge difference between living a fully complete life and simply experiencing it and we want to live every single moment of it as if on a once in a lifetime adventure.

And let's face it, this is in fact our once in a lifetime chance to do this journey, do it right and enjoy it. There are no do-overs.

And as we have embarked on this journey, we are encountering other travelers on their own Third Chapter trek. From folks who spend half the year in their motorhome traversing the country to visit old friends, see new scenery and, most importantly, catch as many shows and concerts in Branson, Vegas, Atlantic City, Tahoe etc as they can to people who now spend much of their time creating crafts and pieces of art.

Fellow travelers who took up scuba diving at age 58 and now explore reefs whenever possible to former corporate executives who now are happily pursuing culinary creative adventures. The scope of what and how you can experience on your own personal Third Chapter is wide, long and only limited to your own personal aspirations and drive. It is fully and completely up to you.

Which brings us to this narrative. We decided that one of the things we wanted to include in our Third Chapter walk was sharing our adventures as well as those of other travelers we meet along the way. The brain experts call it synergy. Something someone else has done may inspire you to try something new. Maybe another traveler is involved in some type of activity or avocation that you never even thought about but all of a sudden it sounds like an awesome idea. And mainly we want folks to know that you don't have to stop. Don't ever stop.

 Gen. Chuck Yeager has a philosophy I have always loved. Don't give up. You may need to take a step back, but don't give up. When he could no longer fly fighter jets he went to prop planes. When he couldn't do those, he went to ultralights. When you can't run a marathon, run a half. Then walk it. Then stroll it....whatever. Just don't quit. Another military motto we try to live by is that we adapt, improvise and overcome.

We have had and we will continue to have hiccups or speed bumps pop up in front of us on this journey, but we are committed to always finding a way around, through or over those obstacles to keep moving forward and make this portion of our lives as full and complete as we possibly can.

So please enjoy the following journey and hopefully you will find your inner Third Chapter self, the buried passion you haven't been able to express before, that special something that will make you jump out of bed in the morning and just go for it. I have mentioned my friend Arsen Marsoobian and you will see him referenced several times in this narrative. One of his favorite phrases is "Add life to your years, not years to your life". Next to leading as complete a life as possible, this, more than anything, is our driving motto.

My Adventure Plan

Mapping out my journey: Mid-term Test

* Where am I right now? (Planning, Preretirement, Retirement)

*

* Mid Term Exam:

> 1 – Have I done what I initially wanted to when I started my work career?
>
> 2 – Did I love, tolerate or hate my job(s)?
>
> 3 – Did I get to go everywhere I wanted to travel to?
>
> 4 – Where did I miss the mark on any of my goals?
>
>
> 5 – What grade would I give myself for success and enjoyment up to this point in my life?
>
>> A – Absolutely everything went right
>>
>> B – Got most of it correct
>>
>> C – Some good, some bad but it evens out
>>
>> D – More downers than ups
>>
>> F – Wouldn't do anything the same again

Chapter One

THE ADVENTURE BEGINS – They Are Called Stepping Stones For A Reason!

"The best way to treat obstacles is to use them as stepping-stones. Laugh at them, tread on them, and let them lead you to something better."

— <u>Enid Blyton</u>

I have discovered an amazing thing as I approach my 60th birthday. OK, maybe more weird than amazing......or scarier.........or just totally different than I expected. I am not 25 anymore. Oh, INSIDE I still pretty much see myself that way but in reality, it just ain't so. I am getting older. According to my kids, a LOT older, but they are still kids....what do they know.

Have you ever just stopped for a few minutes, sat in a quiet place and looked back at all of the events in your life, all the decisions you have made and all of the changes of direction you have experienced and wondered "How the hell did I end up here?" We have done this several times and had in depth conversations about how we got to this point in our lives. So you can understand the context we see things through with our Third Chapter adventures, I need to give you a Reader's Digest version of the roads that we traveled to get us here.

To see the stepping stones we each had to tread on to miraculously reach this point in our lives at the same time. And miraculous it is.

Debbie was born and raised in southern California. I was reared in western Colorado. Debbie was heavily involved in community, Chamber of Commerce, schools, kid sports etc in Moorpark, CA. She grew up and went to school with kids whose parents worked in the film and entertainment industry in Hollywood and LA. She has actually had a couple of different iterations in her life, running the gamut from being among the crème de la crème in town, including a country club life and extensive involvement in community programs, community service groups and school groups to living in a manufacture housing unit (read mobile home) in a gravel pit. She even coached kid's baseball for many years.

I was born and raised in a VERY small town in Western Colorado. The population was about 500 when I graduated from high school. We had the largest graduating class for a couple of years with 36 graduates. My oldest daughter's graduating class in California had almost as many people as the entire town I grew up in did.

 I spent the first major part of my adult life in law enforcement in Colorado, Nevada and Arizona before moving to Central California in 1992. And like Debbie, I had a ton of different experiences and stepping stones ranging from being a business owner to being homeless and living in the local rescue mission homeless shelter.

She moved to the Central Valley in California a couple of years after I did and, as we found out later during our talks, we were involved in many of the same events, groups, Chamber of Commerce programs and other projects. But strangely enough, we never did cross paths.

In 2012 we connected to each other through an online service (yeah, I know, but it worked for us) and we have been together ever since. As we went through all the steps of getting to know each other, talking about our pasts, our plans, our experiences, it became frighteningly clear that each of the stepping stones we each had to travel across, for good or bad, had in some way prepared us for our lives together as we entered into our Third Chapter trek. In some areas of my life and with some of my personality quirks where I was lacking that undefinable "something", Debbie filled in my blanks. And this also works vice versa with her. We seemed to complete each other and ground each other in literally every way we could, and let me tell you, that in and of itself was a scary concept. Scary but also reassuring in so many different ways.

Between us we have had 10 kids and grandchild number 12 arrived in April of 2015. And all of our kids and grandkids are as dissimilar and wonderfully different (eclectic – remember, that is our key watchword) as you can imagine.

We run the gamut from very high maintenance to extremely grounded and practical, almost to the point of being OCD, which being OCD myself, I find reassuring. Although I prefer CDO, which is the correct alphabetic order those letters should be in. But I digress.

 Stepping Stones. Those random life events that help shape our course of travel, our personalities and our relationships. This takes us back to the randomness of life. If I had made one single decision different, changed my direction one little bit, I probably wouldn't have ended up here, with Debbie, experiencing this wonderful Third Chapter adventure that I am. Maybe. On the other hand, because we fit together so well, completing each other's sentences, calling each other just at the time that we needed to talk, having the same ideas at exactly the same time, perhaps we would have ended up here together no matter which path we had taken earlier. That's just one of the questions I have written down to ask God about when I see him. The whichness and the whyness of how people get to where they are going. That and platypuses. I really want to know what the design process was for a platypus.

Stepping Stones. We all encounter them. Some are good, some are bad and some just are. I think we probably don't recognize them or their importance at the time we are crossing them.

Oh, sure we know if it was something really good or something really bad, but I don't believe we fully appreciate the significance of each one at the time they are crossed. I think appreciation only comes in hindsight when you can look back over the turning, twisting path you have taken and then you can see how deeply each step effected your ultimate outcome.

As of this writing, my old high school is planning a multi-year reunion in August. I have been following the planning on the group's Facebook page and over the years I have either maintained or rediscovered friendships with high school pals.

Because of prior, long term commitments, I will not be able to attend this event, but as I have followed the preparations, I have been struck with the realization that the stepping stone path applies to everyone.

From our little high school group in Western Colorado, we now have an attorney, geologists in California, newspaper columnists in large metro newspapers, used car salesmen, farmers, ranchers, oil field roughnecks – we run a huge gamut of life experiences and results. And quite honestly, when I look back at what we were like when we graduated, I would not have been able to predict nor fore see where 90% of us would have ended up. A fair portion of the class still resides with in just a few minutes travel time from the high school while others of us have traveled far and wide and are now about as disconnected from the old home town as you can be.

I remember that when I was growing up, if you met more than a half a dozen cars on the road, it was a veritable traffic jam. Then I remember my first trip into LA. Scared the crap out of me. The LA metro freeway system is enough to turn any outsider into a blithering idiot and I was no exception. Now, having been a Californian for over 23 years, I think nothing of a spur of the moment trip to LA or any of the suburbs and pretty much nothing about the traffic, lifestyle or activity fazes me.

And I cannot help but wonder with this small group of classmates, who are now also entering their own Third Chapter adventures, how they are going to choose to make the journey. How many actually lived a charmed, chosen life and how many still have that inside, burning passion or desire that they have never been able to act on? What twisted and turning path did each of us go down to get to the point that we now find ourselves?

So what were your stepping stones? What events, places or people have you encountered on your life journey to reach your own Third Chapter adventure? I believe we are all pretty much the same in that we have good and bad life experiences and even though each would be drastically different for each of us, there is an underlying commonality that I find reassuring. The biggest thing we have in common is that no matter what each stepping stone was, how we responded or reacted to it is of even greater importance. Did we embrace it and learn from it or did we become angry, bitter and change ourselves in a negative way?

How you have previously responded to stepping on those stones, those trials, will shape how you handle moving into your Third Chapter travels. Will you be open to the new, wonderful adventures that lay ahead or will you be hiding, just knowing that nothing good is coming down the road. It has often been said that what defines us and our character are not the things that happened to us but rather how we responded to those events.

I would hope that your past responses would make you open to choosing the adventure. And I hope these examples of how wonderful a Third Chapter journey can be will help you get up, get right and get moving.

My Adventure Plan

Mapping out my journey: Stepping Stones

* What were my most positive stepping stones?

*

*

* What were my most negative stepping stones?

*

*

* Overall, how did I respond to each of them? Did I take a positive learning approach or did they beat me down and I responded negatively?

*

* What were the 2 biggest life changing events I have experienced?

*

* If I could go back and change just one decision I made during the journey so far, what would it be, why would I change it and what would I have done differently?

*

Chapter Two

How will I know when I have arrived?

"What happens if a man's life is already written? A man must move through life as his destiny wills." –Caine

"Yes. Yet each man is free to live as he chooses. Though they seem opposite, both are true. Choose wisely, Grasshopper"-Old Man

(From the television series Kung Fu)

In discussions with many fellow Third Chapter travelers, one of the main topics that arises is when do people realize that they are in fact starting their Third Chapter. Or that they even have the option of enjoying a Third Chapter adventure. Do they recognize that they are still harboring that certain desire or passion inside that they have never been able to let loose? That they now have the freedom to do anything they have a drive to do? Really, anything?

So, you say you want to have an adventure, to change up things, to fully live this portion of my life. What do I do? How do I do it? All valid questions. And, strangely enough, questions that only you can answer.

I think that discovering your own personal Third Chapter journey is a lot like pain. Not that this part of your life needs to be painful; far from that. It should be one of the most enjoyable parts of your entire existence. My example is this; I cannot judge your pain. If you and I both slammed a finger in the car door, I might drop to the ground in agony, swearing up a blue streak, and you might just shake it off and go "ouch". We all have different pain tolerances and I cannot judge nor relate to yours at all.

Figuring out your Third Chapter is similar to this in that your trip is your trip. We can share our experiences and those of fellow travelers, but in the end, this is your trip, your adventure, your life choices. What you do, where you go, who you go with and how you accomplish all this is entirely up to you. This is good news and bad news all at the same time. Good in that you have an immense amount of freedom at your disposal. Bad because you have an immense amount of freedom at your disposal. You need to choose, well, Grasshopper, to make sure you have the best journey possible.

The first step is very simple. Simple but sometimes not that easy. Just ask yourself the one basic question; what makes me happy? What is the thing that I enjoy the most? Do I even have a passion and if so what is it?

As with most things in life, the answer is usually right in front of us if we just reduce all the ideas, concepts, confusion and options down to one, simple question. What Makes Me Happy?

Remembering that occasionally some things from my prior education do stick with me, I would now refer you to Occam's Razor. This is a decision making theory that states that when considering different options, the simplest is probably the correct one. In other words, KISS it. Keep it simple, stupid. Just go with that gut reaction you feel when you hit upon whatever gets you excited about getting up each morning, what your passion is, what drives you.

A Third Chapter adventure means so many different things to everyone. For us, we want to travel and work a little from the road and have adventures. Simple. For someone else, the journey means finally letting go to that little voice inside that has been denied for years – the one that says you are an artisan. You are so creative and artistic that you have to let go and express yourself through painting or craft designs or woodworking. Whatever makes you jump out of bed in the morning and shout WAZZOO!

Maybe you have been a desk jockey for your entire working life but everyone in the neighborhood just LOVES your cupcakes and pastries. You are a fantastic home cook and baker and you just love doing that. OK, so maybe your Third Chapter adventure is to finally open that little corner bakery and coffee shop you have always dreamed of and keep seeing yourself doing. Then you "knead to rise" to the occasion and bake! (Sorry – one of my vices is an addiction to puns. I will apologize once, but basically you all need to just get used to it – it will probably happen again).

Or maybe you have been a business executive with the three piece suit and a very proper lifestyle your entire professional life but secretly you have watched every episode of Ink Masters and have always had a burning passion for tattoos. Maybe you even have gotten a couple of tattoos that are in easily hidden places over the years but you have always wanted to go full blown gonzo for tats. Go for it. Learn the art. Express yourself. Ink away. Not my cup of tea, but then this is YOUR adventure. I have no room to judge anyone on what they choose to do in their Third Chapter adventure – remember, I suffer from paronomasia (Pun Addict). So as long as it is legal, ethical, won't hurt anyone and satisfies your inner most basic urges, just go for it.

Remember that the road you choose to travel on your Third Chapter Adventure is all yours – you now can own your life and not have to follow the plans or direction of an employer or job requirement. As noted, is some cases, people go off onto a new tangent that is diametrically opposed to anything they have ever done before and sometimes it is just a continuation of whatever they had been doing for the last 25 to 30 years. Again, no wrong answers.

We have been told since we were very young that we didn't need to "reinvent the wheel", that we needed to just follow the guidelines that had been laid out before us and to continue on. Well, your Third Chapter adventure is your chance to "Reinvent" yourself, your life, your outcome.

This is your chance to go do that thing you never got to get to before, to finally pursue your dream or passion in whatever way you want to. And please remember this; it is never too late. I recently saw a line that struck me as very appropriate here, "60 is the new 40" We are living longer and with much improved quality of life so there is no reason not to get out there and go for it.

I recall hearing the story of Sherry Lansing, the former head of Paramount Studios, who when she retired at age 60, started down a completely different journey. Ms. Lansing's mother had died of cancer and because of this she had always supported cancer groups. When she retired, she formed the Sherry Lansing Foundation and now works tirelessly for cancer research and on finding cures.

An unexpected benefit she discovered, aside from the good work she was doing, was that she found herself feeling younger, more alive and more vibrant. The new endeavor made her keep learning new things, push herself outside her normal comfort zone and kept her growing as opposed to just climbing into a golf cart and letting time slip away. But simply thinking about what you want to do, to have a vision or image in your mind of what path to choose, is not nearly enough. You must do two more things. And these are imperative.

First, write it down. Thoughts that we have floating through our minds are just that – thoughts. "Will o' the wisps" as my Celtic ancestors would say.

They have no more substance than a whiff of smoke. However, when you sit down, write down and focus down on what those thoughts, goals and dreams are, then they become real. They become tangible. You can see and touch them. Write down what you want to do or what you want to become and be as detailed as possible. Try to actually put to words all the thoughts and dreams you have had flitting around in your head all these years. And the other part of this is to write them down as goals. Set yourself achievable but specific goals that detail, in writing, specifically what you want to do, how you want to do it and when you will get it done.

Next, and write this down as well, ACT ON IT! I don't remember where I first heard or read this concept, but the basic thought is that NO ONE has ever reached the end of their life and really regretted all the things they did in life. What they really and truly regretted were the things they didn't do. They regretted the opportunities missed, the chances not taken, the roads not traveled. Having the opportunity to pursue your Third Chapter dream is a blessing that in one form or another all of us are provided with. Not pursuing that dream is perhaps the biggest waste of our lives as well as becoming the biggest regret. So we can reduce this to the three simple, basic steps;

1 – What is your bliss? Your Passion? Figure it out and embrace it
2 – Write it down. Lay out on paper what this will look like.
3 – Just Do It. As the Nike ad says.

Many years ago, a fax joke page started being circulated. If you are in your Third Chapter phase, you will remember faxes. For our younger readers, think of a primitive mechanical Facebook where you shared ideas, jokes and cartoons. This one was a picture of a circle with the words "To It" written in the middle. A Round To It. I know, but since it was another form of a pun, it stuck with me. This is what you have to get rid of in your Third Chapter. Lose the idea of "I will get around to it" and embrace the need to "Just Do It". Get off your rear ends, get out of that chair or bed, and go out and live your adventure.

My Adventure Plan

Mapping out my journey: Am I there yet?

* Have I started even thinking about the next part of my life yet?

*

* What are the top 3 things on my Bucket List?

*

*

*

* What is my passion? What activity makes me the happiest?

*

* Which "I will get around to it" do I most regret not doing?

*

* My To Do List:

    * Get a tablet and start actually writing down what I want to do, what my passion is and a time frame I want to accomplish it in.

    * Start writing down ideas as they come to me on ways I can get my journey started, ways I can make this part of my life enjoyable and resources I can use to accomplish this.

Chapter Three

You're going to do what? Are you Crazy?

"It is in the moments of your decisions that your destiny is shaped." Tony Robbins

So getting to this point in your Third Chapter adventure has been all about you and, if it applies, your partner. But there is another dynamic in the journey that you need to be aware of and be prepared to address when it arises. Family. Kids, siblings, possibly parents, friends and other relatives. Pretty much across the board, once you have decided on which course of action is best for you in your Third Chapter experience, not everyone will understand, agree or approve. Our response to our kids and family is simple. Get over it and get used to it. I tell them this kindly and lovingly, of course, but the message is clear; it's our life, our journey, our adventure, so just get over it.

We have experienced the gamut of responses from total support to some folks questioning our sanity. Now for us, our general sanity is always in question, but our Third Chapter decisions are not.

Some of your family members will embrace whatever course you choose to take and give you all the support they can with your decision.

Some will question why you are not making reservations at the closest nursing home or care facility and planning on simply fading into the sunset. Or bugging you about if they are in the will or not. You have a couple of choices to use when dealing with the latter category of people. One, you can simply smile an enigmatic, Mona Lisa type smile, and merrily go on about your business, leaving them to wonder and stew even more. Or you can have The Talk with them and explain that while yes, Grandma and Grandpa are older they are also wiser and the best course of action for them is to embrace life to its fullest and simply blast off into their own adventures. And accept the fact that we are doing what we want to do, the way we want to do it and with whom we want to. In other words, just get over it.

With some of my family, I enjoyed the first response. I simply smile, give them a little all-knowing wink, and go on about my business. Makes them wonder even more. However with most of our family members, we have had discussions about what we do, why we do it and what we have planned for the future. We have found that by being straight forward with all of our kids and grandkids, they understand fully, and in the case of the grandkids, as long as we bring back gifts and trinkets from our travels, they couldn't care less. After all, that's what grandparents are for, to provide cool gifts and activities that mom and dad won't. As you can guess, we are usually pretty popular with this group.

Parents are another matter. Both of Debbie's folks and my mom are still with us and, as is normal with all parents, they worry about us and our choices. And even though there are periodic questions about where we are going and what we are doing, I think they do understand that we are on an adventure that we love and have thought out before embarking on. Also, I think there is just the tiniest bit of jealousy because they never did this and are now at the point where it is not possible to start another adventure. I also think that up to a point, they like to live our adventures vicariously and help satisfy some of their own inner passions. And we are happy to share and include them in with details of all the activities we do.

However you choose to convey it, the message to all of your family and friends is that this is your journey, your passion, your adventure and although you love and care about them, the point of all of this is for you to enjoy your Third Chapter period to the fullest and in the best way that you can. If you are going into some type of new vocation or business, you can possibly fit some of them in to help you with it.

This will not only help them understand the why and how of what you are doing but it can also be an excellent tool in helping deepen your relationship with them. And who knows, you might actually inspire some of them to get their acts together and start pursuing their own passions.

Now while involving family in your adventure is great, up to a point, given the weird minds my kids have (I freely admit they got this from me and my side of the family) I am not sure I would turn them loose in something like a tattoo parlor or a wine shop. I can only imagine the pictures and products these creative but slightly bent minds would come up with. You have to use your own best judgement as to what extent you involve family and friends in your trek. The Prime Directive (Star Trek again– I like to keep the Sci Fi references straight) is to not let anyone be a dream stealer of your goals and plans.

The most important thing to remember is that this is your journey, your experience. We would of course hope that everyone else will understand and support your plan, but if any of them don't, do not let them deter you from your path and goals. We only have a finite amount of time on this old Earth and to spend even one more second of that allotted time doing something we don't have a deep passion for and enjoy to the fullest IS insanity. Don't let anyone take away your vision, your dream just because they can't understand what is driving you.

I recall a conversation with a gentleman at a business conference I was attending. In essence, he was very down, sad and bitter because he had 3 more years to put in at a job he had held for 27 years (and hated) then he had to wait another year until his wife retired from her job.

He had planned it out that they would have 2 to 3 years of puttering around the house in retirement, sell the house, move into a retirement community and simply settle in and await the grim reaper. This was his whole plan and future. I would have been down and depressed as well. This guy had no concept of any other option that was available to him – that he could in fact actually change his direction and have a happy life for once. He was what I call the typical Eyore personality. You all remember Eyore from Winnie the Pooh, the poster character for manic depression? Absolutely everything in and about his life was negative and depressing. If this guy had been with the Wright Brothers prior to their initial flight, he would have said they would never fly. And after they got airborne, he would have moaned that it was now so sad that they would never be able to land.

First I felt sorry for him because he was in essence wasting his entire life and then my feelings changed to anger. Anger that someone would waste all the opportunities for wonderfulness in his life. But most importantly, I realized that I had to get away from this fool as quickly as possible before his attitude became contagious.

And I would encourage you to do the same. As the saying goes, how can you expect to soar with the eagles when you are surrounded by turkeys?

The Law of Attraction states that we attract what we focus on and that by focusing on negativity that is what we attract and experience. Focus on the positive and that's what you will receive. The same goes for your friends and family. Some will get it, some won't and all in all it doesn't matter. Do you get it? Do you embrace your passion? Do you embrace your journey? Then at the end of the day, that is all you need.

My Adventure Plan

Mapping out my journey: They will understand

* Who in my family and circle of friends do I want to understand and embrace my dream and plans?

*

*

* Who will be my biggest supporter(s)?

*

*Who will be my biggest doubters / naysayers?

*

 * What would be my "elevator speech" if I wanted to explain my vision to someone in under 3 minutes?

*

*

* Do I have my vision, plans and goals set firmly enough in my own mind that I can share them and not have someone take them away from me?

*

*

Chapter Four

Being Comfortable in Your Own Skin

"A dream is your creative vision for your life in the future. You must break out of your current comfort zone & become comfortable with the unfamiliar and the unknown."

Denis Waitley

Another old adage is that we grow from discomfort not comfort. In other words, if we stay in the same comfortable place, we will not evolve, obtain more experience nor improve ourselves. Real simple. However, as it is with most things, this is much easier to say than to do. It is called a comfort zone for a reason. WE ARE COMFORTABLE! And we really like being comfortable. We like staying in bed, under the covers on a very cold, rainy day and just turning into a zombie. And we like staying in the same type of comfort zone in our lives. The problem is that when we do this in our actual lives, we also turn into zombies. And we all know what will happen to zombies in the upcoming Zombie Apocalypse.

To put this another way is to borrow a phrase from various 12 step programs. The definition of insanity is doing the same thing over and over and expecting different results; if you keep moving through your life journey on the exact same road you have always traveled you will keep ending up in the same place.

I think that people have a hard time accepting and changing this particular portion of their lives for a couple of reasons. For Baby Boomers, we have a lifetime of believing that we work, we retire, and then we die. Period. The concept of actually having a Third Chapter phase and enjoying it to the fullest is a relatively new idea and sometimes the human mind needs a significant period of time to adjust to the new and uncomfortable.

Even though you have this passion, this desire that has been simmering below the surface of your consciousness for years, when you actually get to the point of putting action to your thoughts, it scares the hell out of us.

Another reason for resisting change is that people are inherently creatures of habit and after a decades long career of doing the work grind day after day in a job that we are so used to that we can do it in our sleep, abrupt change makes us very uncomfortable. And believe you me, I have worked with people that were text book examples of going through life sound asleep. They become so ingrained with the daily grind that pretty soon they are doing everything automatically without ever really thinking about what is going on, what they are doing or where it is all leading.

So now you have come to this gap, a void in your daily existence. You may find yourself in full blown, totally free time retirement or you may be where we are, in that nebulous half in, half out phase where you can see the gap ahead but you aren't fully involved yet. Either way, this is unusual and can be scary as all get out.

The whole idea of having a great Third Chapter experience is that you enjoy it, have a blast, experience a new adventure and just go for it. That is very difficult to do when you are terrified about the journey and insist on still staying in bed, under the covers and staying comfortable. We know this feeling well. There are numerous different emotions you can be feeling as you move into this part of your life and the majority of them are negative and will only interfere with your enjoyment of the experience.

Ok, so now we have identified the problem; great, now how do we deal with it and move on? What can we do to get past the fear and move on? There are several options you have that can help you through this set of 'Stepping Stones" and allow you to move from fear to fun.

One of the first things will be looked at in detail in the next chapter, but for now, you just need to realize that one of the best supports you have to help you adjust are your family and friends. I know, this sounds contradictory to the last section where you had to try to get everyone else to understand what you were doing, but they are also a great source of support for you as you start this adventure. And you have to really communicate; talking is always good, not only good but basically mandatory to continue to grow and get past some of the fear and trepidation that you are experiencing.

I recall the brilliant observation of a friend of mine that he used in 12 step meetings and as a sponsor – your mind is a dark and dangerous place and you must never explore in there alone. Generally, we Homo Sapiens are really good at talking ourselves into or out of mindsets. And sadly it is usually easier to talk ourselves out of doing something than it is to talk ourselves into do something else. Comfort Zone, remember?

If you are in a relationship, either long standing or fairly recent, you have a built in partner to talk to about this experience, what you are feeling, what you want to do and how to go about doing it. Some of you are on solo trips, which is fine, but you do need to find that person or people that you can honestly open up to and share your mindset and fears with. So here is another reference that is going to date me. I think of the conversation from Crocodile Dundee where Sue tells Mick that her friend is seeing a psychiatrist and Mick looks at her, confused, and asks why the friend has to do this. Doesn't she have any "mates"? We all need "mates" as we go through this wild journey called life and whether it is a close partner, family member or friend, we need to have this outlet.

Being as how the vast majority of our fellow Third Chapter travelers are of the same approximate age, we also have similar references and experiences.

Don't misunderstand me, I realize there are differences between someone who grew up in a huge metropolitan area, lived and worked there their entire life and is now looking at this phase of their life from that perspective and someone who comes from a very rural setting, had a totally different work and life style and is coming from an opposite point of view and experience. But there are also significant similarities and those are the points that we each need to embrace and share with each other and with our family and friends. We all need that connection with someone who understands and supports what we are going through.

I will give you the details in the next chapter, but on one of our trips Debbie was able to reconnect with a former business partner that she had not seen for many years and as I watched them visiting, I was somewhat surprised at the speed that they picked up with their relationship just as if no years and distance had separated them. The realization that many of us have a person or people from our past that we can reconnect with and that they will probably be going through the same things we are makes our adjustment much easier. We just need to reach out and make that connection.

This applies if you are doing a solo Third Chapter trip or in a relationship with someone – the result is always the same that making another connection with someone having a similar experience always makes the adjustment much easier. And the whole point of this is to have an enjoyable, happy and wonderful time, not to be stressed about every aspect of your life at all times.

We need to get out of our old comfort zone and become comfortable in our new lives – to become comfortable in our own skin. Another one of those thoughts that are much easier said than done.

Moving from a long established lifestyle into a radically new and different one is scary for everyone and if we let it, this can become almost paralyzing in effect. As I mentioned before, understanding another person's point of view or where they are at emotionally is a lot like sharing pain experiences. Because I cannot actually feel what you are feeling, I cannot truly relate to what you are going through exactly. We cannot know absolutely what each other are feeling as far as fear, excitement, worry or anticipation. But, we can share our thoughts and feelings with others and then help form our own points of reference that will help us deal with our individual journey and emotions. Remember, you don't want to explore the deep, dark interiors of your mind alone; you need to take a trusted traveling companion with you when you make this exploration. Not only is this safer but having another set of eyes, ears and point of view can only help us while we make our adjustments to this new life.

Another great resource for moving from your last phase into your Third Chapter life is to connect with other fellow travelers, those people that you have never met before but when you connect with them, you realize that you are both on the same journey, a new and helpful relationship is formed.

A good portion of our reason for doing this project is to help our fellow Third Chapter travelers connect with each other and help everyone have as great an experience as possible. Plus, we always like meeting new people that have the same focus as us; we continually find that we learn at least one thing (usually a lot of things) from people we meet on our trips and that inevitably this helps us on our own journey. And, I would modestly hope, by sharing our experiences we have helped the folks we talked to as well.

My Adventure Plan

Mapping out my journey: I like me

* What does my current comfort zone look like?

*

* What do I feel most uncomfortable about in moving forward?

*

* What is the biggest rut I am currently stuck in that I need to get out of?

*

* What is my biggest fear moving forward?

*

* What excites me the most about moving forward?

*

* Who are my "Mates" I can best rely on to support me as I move onward with my plans and vision?

*

*

*

Chapter Five

Third Chapter Relationships

"I believe that two people are connected at the heart, and it doesn't matter what you do, or who you are or where you live: there are no boundaries or barriers if two people are destined to be together"
Julia Roberts

As with most things in life, it is better when shared with someone else. For most people. I recognize that there are those individuals that have a wonderful journey all on their own and this is another one of those points where there really is no wrong answer. What is right for you is what is right for you. And by no means do you have to have an awesome partner to travel the Third Chapter road, but for us, it makes the trip so much more enjoyable.

And let me qualify this just a bit. For us, not only having a partner on this journey makes it enjoyable, but having a partner who is just as committed and as focused on embracing the journey makes for an excellent adventure. (My apologies to Bill and Ted. If you get this reference, great. If not, too bad, I am not explaining it.)

Human beings are social animals by nature. We are drawn to contact with others and to have an ongoing connection with our fellow travelers, whether that is with an intimate partner, casual friend or on your own and making new contacts as you travel.

The level of contact that we each personally must maintain is very individualized but the basic fact that we do need social connections is universal.

One of the first things we discovered as we began taking trips and just driving to places is that we really enjoy each other's company and conversation. One evening when we were returning from a business event we were at for Debbie's work, it dawned on us that at no time during our travels had we ever had the radio or a cd on. Even when there were lulls in the conversation, they were comfortable lulls and neither of us felt the urge or need to fill in the blank space with innocuous drivel. We would just have periods of comfortable quiet and then at some point the conversation would resume and we would carry on.

I think that for both of us this was an amazing realization; that you didn't have to fill absolutely every second with some type of forced communication or activity. And I want to reinforce this point – this is our journey. Your adventure is your adventure; everyone is unique has will have a totally different focus and goals.

And in relationships, as is the case with all of your own personal Third Chapter travels, there really is no wrong answer. You may have a long time spouse that you have always been be able to share your life and adventures with. You may be on a solo journey, either by choice or circumstances, and that will be an excellent adventure as well.

And who knows where your individual adventure will lead; possibly that other Third Chapter traveler, soul mate that you haven't even been looking for is just right around the corner. And maybe you are like us. You have found that missing piece to your existence not that long ago and you are now embarking on this journey together.

As I said, there are really no wrong answers. I think the greatest part of this trip is that it holds such an ongoing promise of wonder, excitement and "What if...." What is right around the next bend? Who is going to walk into my shop next? What am I going to see at this next event? What type of awesome surprise is awaiting just around the corner for me?

I know that for us, we have discovered that we love discovery. On a recent trip back to Central California from the coast, we took a little used, two lane highway that I had never been on and Debbie had only traveled once about 20 years ago. We suddenly came around a hill and started down a grade into one of the most incredible valleys either of us had experienced in our travels through the state. It seemed as if each corner we went around opened up an entirely new view and offered a wonderfully different set of scenery. This was really a fantastic trip and we spent the entire time oohing and aahing at each new area as it came into view.

As a further plus, there was also zero cell service; none, nada, zip, so that we did not have any of the usual kid, family, client and office calls that we normally deal with when we are traveling. It was a truly peaceful and serene afternoon and trip.

Now don't get me wrong. I am not telling each of you to pack up and go drive Highway 198 from Coalinga, CA to Salinas, CA and you will have the same experience. You might and you might not. The point is that for each of you, there is a wondrous adventure awaiting you once you get onto your own Third Chapter trek. Having someone to share that journey with is, for us, a great bonus and there is no way either of us would want to have this experience either alone or with anybody else. But that is our reality.

Maybe you are at the point that you are single, enjoy it and just want an adventure. I know of one young lady (she is only in her 70's) who until very recently rode her Harley Davidson motorcycle all over the western United States and had a blast. She made many new friends and saw some amazing country and she was as happy as a clam in the sand doing her journey this way. More power to her.

The only point I would caution you about is that if you are in a relationship or starting a new relationship, is that you should both be in the same place and have the same goals.

Nothing will kill the mood faster than having one partner still working a 40 hour week while the other says "Ta Ta, I am taking off in the camper. Talk to you in a couple of weeks or so. Have fun at work. I will send post cards." This will inevitably result in the end of one relationship and have you starting the quest for another one. Probably not the best way to embark on your Third Chapter adventure.

Friends of ours had to adjust to this themselves. He retired but she still wanted to work a couple of more years. They had started some Third Chapter adventures, extended vacations and the like, but after just a few months, she insisted he return to some type of part time work to keep him busy, out of mischief and, quite honestly, to keep her from killing him as he was driving her nuts being home and wanting to go on adventures all the time. They worked it out so she is taking a little more time off as she goes along and he is working part time to keep from becoming a homicide victim. It worked for them.

Debbie and I are what I would call Tweeners in our Third Chapter adventure. We still have to work but we are winding that aspect of our lives down and incorporating a nomadic Third Chapter lifestyle into our regular routine. We are in a kind of preretirement mode.

After a couple of short, overnight trips in the motorhome, we decided to bite the bullet and take an extended trip just traveling and working as we went.

This was our trial run to verify that we could actually do what we NEEDED to do while at the same time doing what we WANTED to do. I had a business conference in Salt Lake City at the end of April, so we decided to take a week and a half traveling to get there.

Ok, I know you are on the edge of your seats, so I will give you a spoiler alert. It worked great! And we discovered another surprising thing about ourselves and our past travels; we found that even though we were covering a lot of miles, had traffic and construction issues, idiot drivers and unplanned for interruptions, neither of us had been this relaxed and totally non-stressed in a very long time. As we talked about this phenomenon, I began thinking about the differences in this trip and all of my previous travels, vacations and adventures. And the realization hit me that previous trips and travels had all, every one of them, had a very specific and rigid time frame attached to it. Leave point A at this time, get to point B by this time, leave on this date, get to point C here and have just a short time to do some type of activity, then rapidly move onto point D. The end game was to get back home with enough time to get everything ready to get back to work full speed as soon as possible. So what actually happened was that I was so focused on the end of the journey I did not ever actually enjoy the trip itself.

So our first criteria was that we would only work within the barest itinerary we could and mainly just go with the flow. For us, this is an essential part of our Third Chapter adventure.

We had originally planned on leaving on a Monday morning, but because we had everything already to go, we hit the road early on Sunday afternoon and headed to Arizona with the vague idea of getting to somewhere around Kingman before stopping for the night. While we were driving, Debbie remembered that her former business partner now lived in Lake Havasu so she began making calls. Change of plans number one, we went to Lake Havasu and had an awesome evening with Linda and Mike. Even though I had lived and worked as a deputy sheriff in Arizona, I had never been all the way down to Lake Havasu and it had been years since Debbie had, so this unplanned side trip not only let Debbie catch up with Linda, but I got to see the amazing and beautiful country in and around Lake Havasu. None of this would have happened if we had been doing things the old way – having a rigid time table that we just knew we had to follow.

Day two was supposed to get us to Prescott, AZ where I had worked for the Sheriff's Department and I was going to show Debbie around the area, but about midmorning we pulled off I 40, looked at our options and had change of plans number 2 – we went to Flagstaff, got set up at the campground there, unhooked the Jeep and spent the afternoon exploring Oak Creek Canyon and Sedona, AZ.

What an awesome adventure but again, we would not have experienced the special trip down Oak Creek Canyon to Sedona, enjoyed all of the beautiful scenery all the way through to I 17 and had a great drive back into Flagstaff if we had been stuck with a carved in granite itinerary. Also, we spotted one of Debbie's favorite places, a Cracker Barrel, and stopped, shopped and ate, giving us the perfect end to a perfect day.

On the morning of day three, we had initially planned to start across New Mexico, ending up about Albuquerque, but we both woke very early, the Jeep was still disconnected, and we were antsy so we looked and each other and had change of plans number 3 – off we went to see the Grand Canyon at sunrise. This totally unscripted change resulted in one of the most wonderful mornings we have ever had. I don't know if you have ever been able to be on the south rim of the Grand Canyon at sunrise, but take it from us, this is an experience you should all have at least once in your life. We not only got so see one of the most miraculous natural sights in the entire world, but I got to show Debbie deer and elk in their natural environment, up close and personal, which was something she had never had experienced before. And we were also able to plot out ideas for future trips to the area and do a mini bucket list of the other activities we want to do on the next go around.

Over the next several days, we ended up exploring Santa Fe and Albuquerque, NM, Pueblo and Colorado Springs, CO and ended up in Denver, CO to see Debbie's parents. As a side note, we also look upon our adventures as educational opportunities. For example, we learned that you can in fact take a 34 foot motorhome pulling a Jeep Wrangler through the narrow, one lane streets in the Plaza in Old Town Santa Fe. You can, but believe me you are better off taking my word for it and not trying it yourself. I am still not sure which was more interesting to me – the sheer terror of trying to squeeze through those streets or the look of total wonder and fear on the faces of all the people on the sidewalks. I guess it is actually a little bit of both.

After couple of days in Denver visiting with Debbie's parents, we then trekked over the Continental Divide to Grand Junction, CO to visit with my family and we eventually got to Salt Lake City, UT in time for the conference.

During this whole time, we were able to deal with work issues for each of us as they arose, saw some absolutely incredible country, such as the Garden of the Gods, in Colorado Springs, CO, and had a truly awesome time together. So we were able to answer our biggest, most burning question. Yes, we can do this, do it well, and accomplish all we needed and wanted to.

The reason I share this particular adventure is to show that you really need to be on the same page, working towards the same goal as you go through this journey.

If Debbie and I were not in sync with what we wanted to achieve on this trip, all of the changes to the plans that we did, all of the different options that came up that we took, could have made for a miserable experience for both of us. You have to have the same outlook, the same vision as you go down this road. If you are going to be running a specialty business together, traveling, working on community projects or whatever, you need to be totally on the same page.

Again, there are no wrong answers. Your Third Chapter journey will be your own in whatever fashion you want it to be, whether that is in full blown retirement mode or in preretirement as we are. The only mandatory requirement is that you just start your journey in some way.

Baby steps or full blown jump off the diving board and go for it. The how doesn't really matter. The what doesn't matter. The only thing that really matters is that you start. Start it with your soul mate. Start it and find your soul mate. Start it and have a wondrous adventure all on your own. Just Start!

So this is a quick overview of how relationships can work on this journey and in the next chapter we will look at each particular type of relationship you may find yourselves in.

Remember the idea is to make your Third Chapter adventure as enjoyable as possible and if you are fighting issues on the personal or relationship front, you can potentially have a really tough time adapting to this lifestyle change and moving forward.

My Adventure Plan

Mapping out my journey: Relationships

* Define the type of relationship I am in now.

*

* If this is a solo adventure, do my plans include opportunities to meet new people along the way and what are they?

*

* For a couple starting the journey, have we defined our what and how before starting out?

*

*

* As a couple, what are our plans to keep good communications and ensure that we both understand the course we are taking at all times?

*

*

*

Chapter Six

There're Partnerships and Then There're PARTNERSHIPS

"The meeting of two personalities is like the contact of two chemical substances: if there is any reaction, both are transformed."
— C.G. Jung

There are three and only three ways you can travel on your Third Chapter adventure as far as relationships are concerned. That is unless you have perfected time travel or know some aliens that can teleport you around. You will be making this journey either A – Alone, B – With a companion of fairly recent connection or C – With a companion of long standing. That's it; you get to choose one of those three situations and in this chapter we will look at how to make each of these work on a Third Chapter journey. So let us look at each of these situations:

Flying Solo -

If you have reached the jumping off point for your Third Chapter phase and you are doing a solo gig, there is nothing wrong with that. To quote the movie Goodfellas, "It is what it is". What you do need to recognize is that even though you have been alone in your past work life, you have connections that still exist in the form of friends, work associates and family that still provide that social network that all humans require on some level.

You may not have a spouse, girlfriend or boyfriend or significant other, but you do have relationships.

Having said that, one issue that will come up now that you are moving on into your next phase is that only some of those previous connections will remain and stay intact as you move forward. Some of your friends will understand and support what you are doing and some will begin actively discussing putting you in a mental ward; hang onto the first ones and lose the second.

However, another good news part of moving onto your next Third Chapter phase is that you will now have some remarkable opportunities to find and nurture more personal relationships and probably with folks that are more like minded that your past friends and pals.

And unless you are one of those rare 'hermit' minded people, you will find that having someone you can share your adventures with makes it ever so much more enjoyable.

You need to understand that we are talking about two different types of relationships during this time. The first are the up close and personal friends and acquaintances that we can have those heart to heart talks with; the ones that we can share our highs, lows, fears and successes with. The second type ore fellow travelers that we will meet on the way as we go about our own adventures.

These are not mutually exclusive in that a casual friend from work may be going into the same part of his life and you can support each other on your trip and conversely someone you might meet down the road may turn into a very close friend or companion.

Yet another wonderful part of this adventure you are starting out on.

You may be embarking on this journey alone either by choice or by circumstance; you may want to move forward doing a solo gig or you may be actually looking for that special someone to have a more personal relationship with. Either way, the main thing to remember is to just be open to the adventure that lays ahead. Whether you are actually traveling, starting a business, creating art pieces or doing whatever your particular trip is, just be open to the connection opportunities that are around you.

Now if you are just wanting to keep on keeping on and you aren't really looking for a personal connections that is great. Just be open to the friendships you will form along the way. If, however, you are looking for a more personal relationship, this phase of your life can offer you some great opportunities to find that special someone. Depending upon what area of the country you live in, there are normally quite a few "Over 50" singles groups and special interest groups that you can connect with. On line singles and relationship sites are also a good option; I may be biased here because that is how I met Debbie and our adventure is fantastic.

I would offer a word of caution here and this is coming from my past life in law enforcement – basically "Buyer Be Ware". Unfortunately in this day and age of advanced internet and social media resources we also have increased abuse and crime connected with these areas as well. I am sure you can all recall recent stories about people making connections on Craig's List and other online sources that ended up in thefts, robberies or worse. As in most things in life, let common sense be your final rule of thumb and don't let yourself get suckered into a bad situation.

If you are going to try the online connection process, stick with the major dating sites such as Match, Harmony and a really good one for people over 50 called Our Time. The security and control for these sites are much higher than the hundreds of fly by night operations that cover the internet.

We Are Now A Couple -

The next category for our Third Chapter relationships are the recently connected. Debbie and I fall into this group in that we met in August of 2012 and as of this writing are in our third year of the relationship. I would put any couple into this category that has been together less than 5 years because it usually takes about that long to get a relationship clearly defined and established. A lot of the same points that we discussed in the Flying Solo section also apply here, but the biggest difference is that as you meet new people on your Third Chapter journey, you will be meeting them as a couple.

This means that you have to take into consideration the personalities, likes, dislikes and experiences of each of you as you move forward. And this type of relationship will probably be evolving as to what extent you are each involved in the overall process of the adventure. If you are opening up a specialty store, are both of you involved? Are you each going to do something different that appeals to you individually? Are your previous circles of friends and family compatible or not? And as opposed to your initial Third Chapter choices where there are no real wrong answers, here you can have some terrible answers and choices.

The Good Book says that we should not be unequally yoked, which means that we have to have a common focus, goal and desire. Getting out of your old comfort zone and moving into this phase of your life can be scary and difficult at times and if you are in a relationship with someone who is not on the same page as you, that doesn't share your vision, the trip can result in disaster. The biggest asset you have during this time is keeping good, open communications at all time. I know it is an overused cliché, but this is one time where you cannot ASSUME. It will make an ass out of you and me. Don't just figure that your partner has exactly the same vision and goal that you do; you may have had talks about things in general, but you have to make sure you sit down and have regular, ongoing conversation about where you are going, how you are going to get there and to do a regular check up on how you are progressing.

And both of you need to make sure you don't let the other slide in this area. Too often we hear one half of a couple simply respond to the other in general, broad terms of agreement. Things like "That sounds ok" or "I guess so" or, my personal favorite, "Fine". Fine stands for Freaked out, Insecure, Neurotic and Emotional. Avoid this one at all costs.

Another point to be aware of is that as you proceed through this journey, you will each make independent connections and friendships and you need to make sure that both of you are comfortable with them.

I am not saying that both of you need to become BFF's with the same people all the time, but you do need to communicate and let each other know if someone is making you uncomfortable or setting off alarm bells. You both came into this from entirely different backgrounds and life experiences and there is a continuous readjustment process you need to complete as you move forward.

 Simple answer is to COMMUNICATE! The biggest mistakes in communications are those that are never said; don't just assume (there it is again) that each of you is coming to the same conclusion or decision without openly and clearly sharing what your thoughts are.

I can't remember ever not being with you –

The third type of relationships we find in this phase are those couples that have been together for many years, have worked as a team to achieve their goals and reach this point in their lives and who are ready to move together into the Third Chapter adventure. These folks have gotten all the bugs worked out of their relationship, have had all the "should of, could of, would of" questions answered and are moving forward.

I have observed that one of the neat things about being in this type of relationship is that these couples have evolved their own kind of language and communications shorthand. I remember watching a couple in a Denny's a few years ago and for a good 5 to 10 minutes, neither of them actually finished a sentence. One would start to talk and the other would finish the sentence for them; obviously this was their normal communications pattern because neither of them became upset with the other for finishing their thoughts and they just went right along as if this were the most natural thing in the world. Debbie and I are almost there and it is rather cool to have that kind of connection and relationship.

Moving into your Third Chapter as a couple has its own set of challenges just as flying solo does. The biggest and by far most critical item is that you talk during this time. As it is with most things in life, the key is communication, but not just talking; you have to engage in honest and open conversation to make sure each of you are very clear on your vision.

Now you might be one of those other couples that instead of having developed almost an ESP type of communication, you instead have both withdrawn into individual facades and really NEVER actually talk. We know some couples that have, on the surface, a great relationship and all seems right with the world, but in truth, both partners keep so much bottled up inside that their relationship at home when no one is around is tense, stilted and incredibly uncomfortable for both of them. For these people moving into their Third Chapter would be disastrous if they don't get them fixed first.

The biggest suggestion I can give these people is SEEK HELP! The roots for this type of toxic relationship are usually very deep and long standing and you will need some professional help to get out of it. You basically have 3 choices: 1 – Get the heck away from each other and move on with your own lives; 2 – Keep on doing the same things you have always done and continue to both be miserable; or 3 – Get some professional help, get your acts together and over forward in a positive fashion.

I personally believe that for the vast majority of folks the third option is the best – you both saw something and felt something for each other at some point in your past and it's up to you to decide if that something is worth saving and fighting for.

My Adventure Plan

Mapping out my journey: Table for how many?

* Where am I? Solo, New Couple, Long Time Couple?

*

* Flying Solo: What do I want in any relationship moving forward?

*

*

* What resources do I have to help me develop a relationship?

*

*

* For Couples: Are we both clear on the vision and plan?

*

*

* What are the resources we can use to help us develop or maintain good communications and conversation?

*

*

Chapter Seven

I will be the one with the red carnation in my lapel.

"I am always meeting new people and my list of friends seems to change quite a bit" – John Cleese

Hopefully most of you reading this are of a certain age and can remember the old spy and thriller movies where our hero is going to meet a contact in a local bar or restaurant and one of them would be wearing a red carnation in the lapel of his suit so the other person would recognize him. A very simple but elegant way of spotting and connecting with a new person in an unfamiliar setting. When meeting a new client or business referral in a public place, I myself simply tell them to look for a 6'4" bald ex-cop and that I stand out in any crowd. Haven't had anyone miss me yet.

Now, this worked great in the movies, but how do we accomplish this in the real life world of our Third Chapter travels? Here are a few thoughts that have helped us out.

One of the best parts about being on our own Third Chapter adventure is that we are continually meeting fellow travelers in one fashion or another.

Whether it is visiting with another couple in one of the campgrounds we stay at during our longer trips, visiting with the owner of a specialty shop in a strip mall that used to be a CPA and now sells homemade designer soaps, or listening to stories of friends from our pasts that we have recently reconnected with that provides us with some really great examples of people's Third Chapter travels.

Again, here is another area where there are really no wrong answers. Sometimes we enjoy just being the two of us, alone on a back country road or on the shore of a mountain lake and sometimes we have a great time visiting with other Third Chapter Travelers and sharing experiences and stories.

I think that one of the best parts of this trip is that we do get to meet so many new and interesting people and that by listening to their stories we get new ideas of our own, learn about things we had not even considered in our own travels and get to share our experiences with them. This is the synergy I referred to earlier – by sharing thoughts and experiences, we not only help create new ideas for ourselves, but we also help our fellow travelers plug into different projects and activities that they may not have thought of on their own.

But how do you recognize these fellow travelers? In some cases, it is pretty easy. When we pull the motorhome into a campground at the end of a travel day, you can simply look around at the other sites and fairly rapidly figure out who is who.

The site with the slide in pickup camper, 6 bicycles laying outside and 4 kids running around like banshees are probably not fellow travelers. The couple two spaces down that appear to be in their mid-sixties, have a similar motorhome also towing a vehicle and setting up lawn chairs under the awning they just extended probably are good candidates for being fellow Third Chapter-ites. These are the people I want to visit with.

Let's face it, folks. When you reach the point in your life that you are in your Third Chapter, we all have a similar look and presence about us. Regardless of ethnic background, religious belief, economic standing etc we are all going to be in roughly the same age group, have the same slightly amused (or stupefied) looks on our faces and we will be observing everyone else around us to see who else fits in our niche.

These criteria also apply when you enter into a specialty shop or store and find yourself in conversation with the proprietor who also fits into this general classification. Or you are at a county fair, crafts show or similar event and visit with a booth that has custom wines, wood carved signs, home grown lavender products or whatever, you might just be meeting some fellow Third Chapter travelers. And let me pass along the most prominent self-truth for Third Chapter travelers....the vast majority of us love to talk. We want to share our experiences.

We want to find out where the folks next door have been and what they have found on their journey. We want them to share the good, the bad and the ugly about their adventures. Firstly, because we are genuinely interested and secondly, if someone else has already found out about a pitfall or screwed something up, we would rather learn about it in conversation than to experience it ourselves. Sort of a self-preservation thing. Also it's an "I don't want to look stupid in public" thing. I know you all can relate.

One of the best parts about having these conversations is that you can always pick up a little nugget or two. Anything from seeing a better way to stow an electric cord in the motorhome to finding out about an entirely different life path that you would never have chosen. Like opening a tattoo shop. I mean you just never know.

What? You have a lavender farm where your grow incredible lavender plants and you travel the country going to county fairs and home shows, selling your products, traveling and seeing the country all at the same time? WOW!

You took up scuba diving when you were how old? And survived? Now you make 4 to 5 trips a year to different reef areas and explore the undersea world? But you were a geologist in your old life – how the heck did you turn into Jacques Cousteau?

Ok, so let me get this straight. You were a corporate executive for 25 years, three piece suits and 2 hour business lunches.

But you have now learned to weld and all of these awesome metal statues are your creations? I really want to know how that transition worked!

I firmly believe that the old adage that you don't know what you don't know really applies to our Third Chapter adventure. You may discover some brand new connection or idea that you had never considered before. You may discover a whole new group of friends and likeminded individuals that you would never have thought about having a relationship with before. The neatest thing about your Third Chapter trip is that it can truly be a full blown adventure. The choice is yours.

And just like making the decision on what to do and how to do it, making connections with fellow Third Chapter travelers is a conscious decision and also requires action. Getting back to your home and thinking, "Man, those folks that run that wine store looked like they were having fun", means that you missed the boat by not engaging them in conversation. Why didn't you ask them how they got into that business? What sparked their need to go down that particular road on their Third Chapter travels? This also requires action on your part even if that means getting out of your comfort zone and pushing yourself. And let me tell you I know that is scary. But we do not grow if we do not challenge ourselves. The only way we will ever expand our universe is by experiencing it, embracing it and challenging ourselves to go forth and explore, ask questions and appreciate the adventure.

There is an old joke about a 12 step program being formed for procrastinators anonymous. But no one ever got around to actually starting the group. I think the saddest people I can ever remember meeting are the ones who have told me "I always meant to do that." I distinctly recall the faces of people I have talked to about our adventures and seeing the light come on in their eyes as they realize how awesome and cool it is to have experiences like this. Then the light dims and they inevitably look at me and say something to the effect of "That sounds like it was incredible. I always meant to do that." They use that same old approach that they will get around to it. Someday. Probably.

And another thing we have learned is that when we encounter these types of people, we get the heck away from them as fast as possible. I think negativity is even more infectious than measles or small pox. If you let someone else's Dark Side begin to invade your Positive Force (Star Wars for you uninitiated) then you begin to travel down that road and not on the path you are supposed to be taking.

Again, thanks to our modern world of the internet and social media, you also have a vast array of resources to use to make these connections. There are any number of specialty groups available online for the over 50 crowd and they cover the entire range of interests from starting a business to planning exotic vacations. In many areas, you can also find smaller groups that meet in person on a regular basis that are comprised of folks with similar interests and experiences.

One more oldie but goodie adage is that as big as the world is, it is still a very small community; you don't know who you will run into in some of the most distant places from home. Acquaintances of ours took off in their RV for a month long leisure trip through the western U.S. and ended up going into Canada and stopped at Glacier National Park. When they climbed out of their motorhome, a familiar voice yelled at them and asked what the heck they were doing so far from home. Another couple from home, whom they had not discussed their plans with, happened to be in the exact same park, at the exact same time, looking at the exact same scenery. Like I said, it is actually a very small world.

The only thing that makes total sense to me is for each of us to approach own individual Third Chapters with as much gusto and excitement as we can. It really doesn't matter what we do, how we do it, how extravagant we get or what particular activities we become involved in. The ultimate goal is to reach the final end of our journey and to have nothing we could look back on and say "I always meant to do that."

My Adventure Plan

Mapping out my journey: Getting Connected

* Who do I want to connect with? What interests do I want to talk to someone about?

*

*

*

* What are my global (Internet etc) resources?

    * Online special interest groups?

    * Online social groups?

* What are the local group meetings I have access to?

*

*

*

* Who in my current circle of influence can be a resource?

*

*

Chapter Eight

OK, so now how does this work?

"If you don't know where you are going, you are going to end up someplace else." Yogi Berra

Another favorite Yogi Berra quote..... "It ain't over til it's over"..... Or maybe it was Casey Stengel. One of those great philosophers. Anyway, the point is we all need some kind of map. Some type of directions to help us get from point A to point B. And if you don't have that map, then you will likely end up at point J, and who wants to end up there! So one of the more important things you need to have as you enter into your own Third Chapter adventure is a map, a plan, a set of goals that you want to follow to reach your next destination. And understand that goal setting or trip planning is not an end all by itself but rather just more stepping stones along the way. Once you reach one goal, one plateau, then set your sights on another one – keep moving forward and keep your eyes on the next object and look at each goal you hit as one more rung on the ladder.

People generally move into their Third Chapter with a very similar set of requirements but different visions, which is to be expected as we are all totally different individuals.

There are basically four similar requirements we all possess that each of us can relate to:

We Want –

Intellectual Stimulation – we need to keep learning, to experience new things and to have fresh ideas so that we continue to feel fully alive.

Financial Security – we also want to do two things, pretty much in conjunction with each other: Make sure we have enough income to keep moving forward and to be as responsible with our spending as we can.

A meaningful life – we want to do something meaningful during this Third Chapter adventure. By meaningful I mean doing something that helps someone else, which helps some group; that makes a positive impact.

Have fun – Our Third Chapter journey needs to be fun. We need to enjoy the trip as well as the end result.

We entered into this adventure with a pretty clearly defined series of stages we want to reach. The first was to get a residual income coming in each month that would replace our combined regular income and allow us to transition into full time Third Chapter living. The second phase is to work while traveling and continue our adventure while at the same time ensuring we are building the retirement funding.

And the last part is to fully retire from work and just do US time, whether that is traveling, puttering around the house, spending times with the kids and grandkids, or seeing friends and just generally have a wonderful adventure.

Whatever your goals are, wherever you want to go and whatever you want to do, the plan is really simple to reach them. Notice I said simple, not always easy. We have found that actually writing down our hopes, dreams, plans and goals makes them real. You will find it much easier to focus on them is you can actually see them. Visualization Of The Cosmic All, as one of my favorite Sci Fi novels says.

Your own personal Third Chapter goals should be very simple and easy to identify. What makes you happy? What is your passion? Where do you want to go? Who do you want to do all of this with? Just sit down in a quiet place, let your mind roam free and simply ask yourself "What would make me the happiest at this point in my life?"

It is really a simple, two-step process:

#1 – Figure out what you love to do and #2 – Go out and do it. Period.

Like I said, simple. Maybe not real easy, but simple. The first hard part is figuring out the What. You need to just listen to your inner self and let your head and heart be fully open.

Now just look for that passion, that desire, that "something" that makes your heart go pitty pat and makes your brain go aahh! Is it doing something to turn loose that creative, childlike side of yourself such as painting, building furniture, learning welding and making unique statues?

I believe that everyone has some kind of personal passion that they keep in a quiet, secret place in their minds that they periodically go back and visit, doing the "someday" dance in their head. And some of the most deeply ingrained ideas belong to some of the most unsuspecting people. I recall a story about a high ranking law enforcement official an associate of mine had worked with. He was a consummate professional and was held in high esteem by everyone he worked with. If you looked up the words professional and proper in the dictionary, that was him.

On an extended training trip one time, he confided to my friend that he had a personal passion that he had never acted upon and really didn't think he would ever be able to. Turns out that as a very young man, he had a relative that had been in the Navy and who had a somewhat dubious collection of tattoos he had accumulated over the years. These always fascinated him, but being as he had always know he was destined for a career in law enforcement, he had never acted upon this attraction. He was fascinated by the process, the creativity and the art required to do quality, professional tattoos. But he had never done anything about it.

When last heard from he had retired from the department and was now happy as can be running his own tattoo parlor and he himself has just about finished full sleeve tats on both arms. Go figure. Again, not my thing (I hate needles) but it isn't my Third Chapter journey, it is his.

Maybe you are a frustrated Hemmingway or J.K. Rowling with the next great American novel rambling around in your head. You know you have a great story to be told and you would love to share it with the world, but you think it is just one of those things you only dream about. Nuts. Sit down, plan it out and write your book. Even if it is never published or no one reads it, who cares? The point is that you satisfied that internal itch...you wrote a book! Now just how cool is that?

Or, just maybe, you have always wanted to run some type of specialty business – if you have always had a passion for wines, maybe now is the time to open that little custom wine tasting and sales shop. Maybe you have always harbored a deep secret desire to learn clowning and become a party clown for kid's parties. It really doesn't matter because it is YOUR dream. YOUR passion. YOUR desire. But you need to fully realize the What then you can move on to the How.

Figuring out how to do your How is not as easy as the What. This part does require some careful thought and some specific planning, but as we have found, this in and of itself can also be a really fun part of the process.

A long time precept in motivational and positive thinking is that writing it down makes it clear and makes it real. One of the best ways I have found over the years is to just get a new writing tablet and just start writing. Whenever something hits you, write it down, in no particular order, just write it down. You can go back and organize the thoughts but the first step is to just get the thoughts out of your head and onto paper. Another way is to use a PostiNote pad and a bulletin board to jot down thoughts and ideas and then just stick them onto the board. Again, you can go back at any time and put them into a rational order, but the goal is to just let your brain have a freewheeling outlet to move the thoughts and ideas out of your head and onto paper.

Once you have figured out the What and the How there is really only one thing left to do. ACT on it. All the dreaming, wishing, thinking and planning in the entire world accounts for absolutely nothing if you do not also include action. Now you may need to take this action in stages, like Debbie and I are. Baby steps. Work out the bugs as you go along but take those baby steps; not moving forward is exactly the same as moving backward.

If you want to become a baker, start working on your book of recipes, take business courses, take cooking courses and map out your plan. Start small and start peddling your wares to friends and neighbors and build up to a regular business. A couple of ladies I know have made a wonderful career out of having a mobile coffee and pastry truck that visits office complexes every day. It doesn't matter what you do as long as you do something.

Want to eventually open a little niche wine shop? Start making connections at local wineries. Study up on all the intricacies of the industry. Take the baby steps but just start.

Now you must also understand and appreciate that you do not need to start this adventure all on your own. Sure, the decision about what you want to do and how you want to get there are all yours, but you do have a ton of resources out there to help you on this path.

If you have had a blue collar job all of your life and now you are looking at opening a specialty business or shop, there are resources available through the public library, local small business development centers, your local Chamber of Commerce, adult schools and colleges in your area, and national groups, such as AARP, that you can access on line for assistance and guidance.

If you are looking for assistance in getting any type of program or project started, you will be able to find many resources locally, from art clubs and galleries that can help you connect with fellow artisans to get your creativity juices flowing to business consultants that will help you get the actual nuts and bolts of running a business together. The answers are out there, you just need to look for them and this startup phase can be as fun and exciting as the actual journey once you get started.

Say you want to travel full time, that you are done with mowing lawns, doing repairs around the house, being tied down to a piece of property and you just want the freedom of the road.

Sort of an old "Ride the rails" hobo type existence, but you just cannot afford to buy an RV and just hit the road. There is a wonderful new lifestyle that is just now becoming more and more accessible – it is called Workamping. Basically, there is an entire community of likeminded individuals and RV parks & campgrounds that will give you a space and pay you wages to work in the campground while living there. When you are ready to move on, locate the next facility on the road you want to travel down and move your rig there and continue working while traveling. This is a very unique and interesting concept but it only goes to prove that no matter what your dreams or desires, there is a way out there to make it work for you.

We mentioned in the preface that there would be opportunities to connect with fellow travelers and to become involved in this growing community. Specific details will be in the last chapter, but in our ongoing effort to connect people together and share our varied stories and experiences, we are currently laying out a second publication that will follow a format similar to "Chicken Soup For The Soul" in that you and all of our other fellow travelers can submit individual stories and experiences to share with the community as a whole.

We are also in the process of completing a web site that will be used to provide information for other Third Chapter community members to share information on business opportunities, travel and vacation recommendations and experiences, hobby and craft tips and suggestions and much, much more.

Another portion of this community we are working on establishing is that we want to create a type of mentor program where fellow travelers with experiences in areas you need assistance and information about can be available to assist you as you go into your Third Chapter adventure.

Additionally, we have included just a small, partial list of online resources available to you in several of the areas we have discussed. This is only a representative sample of what is out there based upon your individual goals, passion and desires. Just be assured that there is help available.

Resources

For basic information on how to start any business and entrepreneur programs:

www.score.org – this is the web site for the Service Core of Retired Executives. This is an awesome resource where you can connect with retired business executives from virtually every business and industry you can imagine and obtain specialized assistance for your own personal project.

www.aarp.org – the American Association Of Retired People has lots of specialized links and referrals for all aspects of starting a new business or unique endeavor.

www.irs.gov/Retirement-Plans/Plan-Sponsor/Small-Business-Retirement-Plan-Resources- - yes, they are from the government and they are here to help you. This site is a good resource for questions about regulations and requirements for specific enterprises.

https://www.sba.gov/content/50-entrepreneurs – the Small Business Administration maintains a library of great connections to assist you in about any area of concern.

http://www.inc.com/jeff-haden/60-great-tools-and-resources-for-entrepreneurs-and-startups.html – Inc. Magazine has great articles and resources not only online but through their publication as well.

http://www.forbes.com/fdc/welcome_mjx.shtml – Forbes Magazine is a long time recognized authority on business related matters and resources.

http://www.entrepreneurship.org/ - just a general over all great site for budding entrepreneurs.

For information on artistic, creative and hobby focused activities:

http://www.outpostartistsresources.org/

http://www.artistcommunities.org/programs/artist-resources

Baking and food service industry connections:

http://www.asbe.org/resources/national-bakery-associations-and-resources/

http://thebakersguide.com/resources

Information on how to start and open different types of wine and wine related businesses and shops.

http://www.new-wine.org/resources

http://www.bplans.com/wine_store_business_plan/executive_summary_fc.php

http://smallbusiness.chron.com/things-before-opening-wine-store-23801.html

And just because I find people's interest in this so fascinating, here is a great link for you wanna be tattoo artists. Enjoy!

http://smallbusiness.chron.com/start-tattoo-shop-12937.html

The astute reader will have learned by this time that our specific journey involves a lot of travel and adventure, the majority of which is in our motorhome. So a lot of our focus is on this area. Here are some exception links for those of you who are also in the travel an adventure mode:

www.koa.com – while none of these links are from a compensated endorsement, we would personally highly recommend the KOA system. They are doing an excellent job of updating and modernizing all of their facilities and we stay with KOA whenever possible. Additionally, KOA is looking for new business partners and franchisees on a continual basis and if any of you other traveling Third Chapter folks might be considering this lifestyle, this might be an option for you. Again, we don't get paid to say this, it is just our best recommendation based upon our personal experiences.

http://hotelguides.com/

http://www.nationalparks.org/explore-park

http://www.reserveamerica.com/campgroundDirectory.d

http://www.goodsamcamping.com/

http://www.wheelersguides.com/

As I noted earlier, these are but just a very few of the options available to you online to explore your individual interests and requirements. And because everyone's Third Chapter journey is so distinctly individual and unique, I am sure some of you will have questions in any number of other areas of interest. Just rest assured, that the resources and assistance you need are out there. You only have to look for them.

Lastly, let us give you just a short list of some areas of interest that might jog that primal part of your brain and get you thinking about what you can do to reinvent yourself at this time of your life:

BUSINESS:

Wine Shop	Greeting Card / Gift Shop	Business Consultant
Antique Store	Sports Memorabilia Shop	Specialty Food Market
Rare Collectables	Party or Event Organizer	Bakery

HOBBY AS A BUSINESS:

Fishing Guide	Painting – Art Gallery	Welding – Sculptures
Collector (Comic Books, Stamps, Door Knobs, whatever)		Specialty Shop
Photography – Studio	Travel – Travel Writer	Reading – Author

RECREATION:

RV Travel	Tent Camping	Photography
Hunting	Hiking	Landscape

Basically if you can think it, you can do it. For example, here is an idea I had shared with me as a Third Chapter vision for one couple. The idea was to outfit a large 5th wheel trailer with the back half as a photo studio, you know the kind with old west and antique costumes etc and a sepia lithograph camera and the front half as a living area and then tour the country, working county fairs and events. This way they could see a lot of country, meet tons of new people, pay for everything as they went and just generally have a blast. Now THIS is a magnificent Third Chapter adventure!

My Adventure Plan

Mapping out my journey: How does this work?

* Here is my "Map" – Write it down

*

    * What is my "What"?

    *

    * What is my "How"?

    *

* What do I want to learn?

*

*

* What do I want to share?

*

*

* Who can I connect with right now to help get me started?

*

*

Chapter Nine

He ain't heavy, he's my brother!

"From what we get, we can make a living; what we give, however, makes a life." ~ Arthur Ashe

We have always believed that one of the reasons we are here during our time on Earth is that we are also supposed to help others as we move through our own lives. The how, why and how much is something each of us must decide individually. But at some level, by helping others, by easing someone else's load a little bit, we live better ourselves.

As far as our Third Chapter life goes, there are vastly different levels of involvement but after having had a full, successful life to this point, it only makes sense to want to pass on some of our experience or encouragement to others. And, as with all things in this adventure, your decision is your decision – there are still no wrong answers.

Earlier I mentioned Sherry Lansing, the former Paramount Studios president, started a non-profit cancer research foundation and worked towards its success full time. That's her journey.

Now maybe you are in a position where you can just commit to a non-profit or charity full time and that will become your entire Third Chapter journey.

For the majority of us, however, we probably are not in that place and will need to work our sharing & caring plan as a part of our overall Third Chapter life.

As an example, I work with a riding academy that provides horse therapy for disabled people, both with riding activities and with contact therapy. One of the volunteers here is a retired nurse who donates a couple of days a week to help with the kids. This is her sharing and caring outlet.

Just as in our regular activities, we tend to be drawn to groups and activities that are consistent with our own experiences, interests and connections so it is not surprising that when we begin to give back, we have similar attractions. You may have been involved with some program or group that already speaks to your need to give back or you have not had this opportunity yet and are now looking for that "thing" to connect with that will satisfy you in that special way.

Just like when you were looking at what to do during your Third Chapter journey, the number of groups and programs you can get involved in with giving activities is vast and varied. And just like choosing your Third Chapter life, you need to pick a program to work with that also holds great interest and satisfaction for you personally.

Debbie and I each have very personally connected experiences in this area. Debbie has a granddaughter and I have a daughter who are special needs kids.

We both have a type of automatic mind set when we are going about our daily lives that always allow us to look for connections and resources for programs the girls are involved in. In other words, we have a specific focus based on our experiences that dictates the type of programs we look for and become involved in.

Perhaps you had a family member or friend that had to battle cancer so you would be drawn to working with some type of cancer research or support group. Maybe you had some real challenges with a kid or kids when they were younger and you want to help out with a group like Big Brothers / Big Sisters.

Or maybe you have a much more personal connection. With a large portion of our population having some type of addiction issues (alcohol, drugs, eating, gambling or whatever) it is reasonable to assume that a good portion of you have experience with addictions either directly or as a family member of an addict. I myself have been involved in Gamblers Anonymous since 1989. My point is that we can usually find programs that need our help and that speak to us on some very personal level.

So once you figure out your own what and why, then you need to settle on your how. For some of us that might be financial support; for others, you may want and need to have a more direct, hands on involvement. Either way works as long as you just get involved.

Be aware of one pitfall in deciding which or what type of community action you want to be involved in, if any at all. Your honest intent is more important by far than any concrete action or activity you will do. By that, I mean you should deeply and truly want to be involved in the sharing and caring outlet and not just do it so that you look good to others or because you think it is something you should be doing. I remember a gentleman at a men's group a few years ago who when asked why he chose one particular church said that he drove around town for several Sundays in a row looking at what type of cars were parked at each church. He settled on one that he felt had the highest number of expensive luxury vehicles and assumed that this would give him the greatest opportunity for connections and networking to increase his own income.

He never looked into what the church was about, what programs they had, nothing other than if he thought it would help him personally.

The same thing applies to giving back. If you are only selecting a program or cause to connect with people you think can help you and not vice versa, then quite simply Don't Do It. Do us all a favor and just go about your regular routine and enjoy your own Third Chapter trip however you may.

My Adventure Plan

Mapping out my journey: How can I pass it on?

* What volunteer areas interest me?

*

*

* What talents and skills do I have that are needed?

*

*

* How much time can I donate or give?

*

*

* Who do I know that is already giving back?

*

*

* What group or organization do I want to work with?

*

*

Chapter Ten

I see how it works but how can I do it?

"Life is either a daring adventure or nothing at all."
— Helen Keller, *The Open Door*

We fully realize and appreciate that all of us are coming into this phase of life from totally different backgrounds, professions, economic status and experiences. Our fellow Third Chapter travelers include corporate CEO's that had six figure incomes and lived in large metropolitan areas to blue collar folks who worked in a factory or drove a truck all their lives and who are coming into the adventure from polar opposite directions. And my response when asked about this is "I don't care. So what?"

You will recall Gen. Chuck Yeager's philosophy I shared early on in this book that you never give up. You may have to take steps back, but you never give up. That is what our individual Third Chapters are all about. It doesn't matter if you have $100 or $1,000,000 in your bank account when you get to this point of your adventure; the only thing that matters is that you embrace your own individual Third Chapter and simply go for it.

Set a realistic budget and live within it, of course, but at whatever level you need to work at, just get going and do it.

You may need to start with baby steps; small, incremental phases as you move forward or you may be in a position where you are jumping into a full retirement Third Chapter life with both feet. Once again, there are no wrong answers – your journey is your journey and you cannot compare what you experience to anyone else. Earlier we reviewed just a few of the resource options available to you either online or in your local community and you need to understand that this list is very basic. If you need help, information or assistance with just about any subject or area you want to delve into, there are solutions available to you.

I remember seeing a quote from Randy Pausch that I found very helpful and inspirational as we started our journey. I share it with you now.

"The brick walls are there for a reason. The brick walls are not there to keep us out. The brick walls are there to give us a chance to show how badly we want something. Because the brick walls are there to stop the people who don't want it badly enough. They're there to stop the other people."
– Randy Pausch, *The Last Lecture*

We discussed earlier how Debbie and I have been pleasantly surprised to find that going through the process of planning and preparing for our own adventure is every bit as much fun and satisfying as the actual journey is.

I think that the reason for this is that we can feed the vision we have in our minds about what we are going to experience and this in turn helps keep us motivated, on course and enjoying the heck out of the experience.

The other result of going through this process, facing our challenges and getting over those next stepping stones is the immense feeling of satisfaction and accomplishment that we feel each time we conquer another step. I am not sure that we would appreciate our adventure quite as much if we'd had the whole package just handed to us without having to make any personal investment or put sweat equity into the program. And by building our own Third Chapter world as we go, we are maintaining a large amount of control and management on the direction we go and the results we get. Remember that the very first step is that image, that vision in your mind's eye where you can very clearly see what you want to do and how you want to get there.

One of the most successful computer salesmen I ever met never turned on a computer nor did he do any demonstrations. When I asked him how this was possible, he explained that what he did when he was talking to a new customer was to simply talk to them about what their level of experience was, what they want to accomplish and how they wanted to use it. Then he would paint the picture in their mind of what they would experience with the new system. By planting this image in their minds, it immediately became more real and much more a positive reflection of what they were actually seeking.

We can use this same approach with our Third Chapter planning. We discussed earlier the need to write our goals and plans down to make then very tangible. The next critical part of this is to then just see in your mind what this adventure will look like. Picture that little corner bakery and coffee shop in your head. See what the display cases look like, smell the fresh muffins and cupcakes, take in the aroma of the fresh brewed coffee. Let it become part of you.

Another concept that has been around for a while and is gaining in popularity today is The Secret. I will let you explore all of the intricacies of this phenomenon yourselves, but for now what we will look at is the basics of this idea and how it applies to your Third Chapter journey.

In its simplest terms, The Secret says that if you create a visual Dream Board with photos of your ultimate dreams and desires on it and regularly focus and meditate on it, those things will manifest themselves in your life. This is in conjunction and part of the recognized idea of The Law of Attractions which says that what we focus on, what we fixate on is what we attract and what will be delivered to us.

There is a huge difference between just wishful thinking, random day dreaming or fantasies about what you would like to do if you ever "get around to it" and having a focused, written, well thought out and very visual example of what your journey and destination look like.

The first is just a "Maybe someday - that would be nice" and the second is a focused "This is what I am going to do, how I am going to get there and what it will look like when I arrive there".

I guess the best way to put this is that you need to achieve a total sense of conviction about what your passion is, how you want to satisfy that passion and what your individual journey and results will look like. Know it, Live it, Love It, Breath it. This belief should become as much a part of your life as breathing in and out; it becomes totally natural, normal and fully a part of YOU.

My Adventure Plan

Mapping out my journey: How can I do this?

* What is the clear, big picture in my mind of my Third Chapter life?

*

*

* Have I written down my plan and my goals?

*

*What are the first 5 steps I need to take to get started?

*

*

*

*

*

* What resources do I need to tap into? Who can help me get my Third Chapter plan in place and get started?

*

*

Chapter Eleven

Connections, Connections, Connections!

"Sometimes, reaching out and taking someone's hand is the beginning of a journey. At other times, it is allowing another to take yours."

— Vera Nazarian, *The Perpetual Calendar of Inspiration*

Now that we have figured out what exactly the Third Chapter of Life is, what your individual passion is, how you are going to start your journey and what you can expect, the next thing we need to do is to establish our connections. Gather Our Collective Consciousness. OK that is a little grandiose – let's just say, Come on People, Let's Get It Together!

We recently became aware of another motivational trend that is becoming more popular all of the time. It is called the Semi Colon. This is based on writing, actually, but it also applies to our lives and in particular, our Third Chapter travels.

When a writer reaches a point in a sentence that he wants to introduce a new or slightly different idea, he has two choices. First, you can just drop in a period and start a new thought. Or you can use a semi colon, pause, and then continue with a slightly different track.

Many people are now having a tattoo of a semi colon put on the inside of one of their wrist to remind them that it is ok to pause, to reconsider and think about the next steps, but that it is only a pause. The key is that you then start up again and keep going.

I think this very aptly applies to our Third Chapter journey. We have reached the point in our lives that we need to put in a semi colon, pause for just a bit, get refocused and then move forward with all the excitement and enthusiasm we can muster. We need to move forward boldly, with common sense and a plan of course, but move forward in a determined manner none the less.

As I related in the beginning of this book, one of the things Debbie and I wanted to accomplish was to help create a network of fellow Third Chapter travelers and to establish some form of community where there can be a free flowing process of sharing thoughts, ideas, plans and experiences. Kind of a brain trust for those of us on this journey. From an initial small idea on how to connect with others, the concept has grown in to a multi-facetted process. The first step was the creation of this simple but concise (I hope!) book explaining our vision and ideas.

The second step is to start to accumulate stories and anecdotes from other Third Chapter people on their own choices, good decisions, bad decisions, experiences, ideas, vocations and vacations. The idea is to put together something along the lines of "Chicken Soup for the Soul" with short stories coming from the entire Third Chapter community.

The last section of this book will have contact and connection information so that you can become better connected with other travelers and hopefully enhance not only your individual journey but theirs as well.

And we want to hear your stories. We want to learn and share what our fellow travelers are doing; what awesome ideas have you had, what opportunities have been presented to you. What have you learned that you want to share with others?

Next is to create and run an online presence through an open web site and Facebook page that will give our fellow travelers instant access to information such as great vacation ideas; good or bad restaurant, hotel, campground or vacation site experiences; ideas for businesses and vocations that work or don't work and a myriad of other issues that everyone would benefit from having access to.

Part of this would embrace the Third Chapter community and create forums where likeminded entrepreneurs can also share business and project ideas, successes, failures and connections. As mentioned earlier, we are big on using synergy to help create growing and positive relationships and environments.

And lastly, I would like to eventually have regional convention type get together meetings / conferences where all of you like minded individuals can actually come together face to face, share experiences and ideas and make the personal relationships that are so much a part of going through similar journeys.

Social media is a truly great and wonderful resource but we still believe there is nothing like actual personal and direct contact with other members of the human race to help build our own excitement and positive environment. We can easily envision having numerous regional group gatherings that can focus on specific areas of interest as well as each person's individual Third Chapter adventures. And another positive aspect of these programs is that you don't know who or what you don't know. What if during a chat about a personal creative project you were involved in you were suddenly exposed to a totally different idea or concept that you had never considered before? What if a person you have just made a connection with suddenly turns on a light for a business idea that had never crossed your mind before meeting them? And what if you are on that solo journey and suddenly you meet "The One" person you have been looking for?

Lots of "What If's". But in reality, that is the final beauty of being on your Third Chapter adventure – the adventure itself. The wide open opportunities that lay before you that you now have the chance to go and explore. All of the wondrous What If's that lay ahead of you. Kind of gives you goose bumps just thinking about it, doesn't it?

My Adventure Plan

Mapping out my journey: Making my connections.

* What connections do I want to make?

*

*

* What are my top 3 questions on doing my own Third Chapter adventure that I need help with?

*

*

*

* What is the biggest adventure or event that I have experienced so far that I want to share?

*

*

* What is the biggest "I wish I could do that" thing you want to do?

*

*

*

I LOVE IT WHEN A PLAN COMES TOGETHER!

"Plan for what is difficult while it is easy, do what is great while it is small."   Sun Tzu

We hope that this has been a help to you as you start the planning and implementation of your own Third Chapter adventure. This is truly a once in a lifetime opportunity because we only have this one shot for our time here and I believe we should make the absolute most of it that we can. So here is what YOU have to do now:

1 – Figure it out. Do that deep soul search and find out what your Third Chapter dream is. Identify what your passion is and what will simply make you happy.

2 – Write it down. Seeing your plan in black and white, written down, makes it real. It becomes tangible and real to you so that you can fully embrace who you are and what you want to do.

3 – Make a plan and then work that plan. Goals and plans without action are merely dreams. Don't just talk about it but rather get off your cans and get out there and do it.

Here is to an awesome Third Chapter adventure for you and we look forward to hearing about your own experiences. Eric and Debbie

JOIN THE COMMUNITY!

Calling all Third Chapter Travelers – we are looking for stories and tales of personal experiences from all of our fellow adventurers. If you have any type of story to share, either about a business opportunity or experience, some type of leisure adventure, a community involvement program.....whatever is important to you, share it with us.

Facebook Groups – Third Chapter Adventures

Go to www.thirdchapterlife.com

OR

Email us at info@thirdchapterlife.com

OR

Call us at 559-300-2303

ISBN-13: 978-1512378412
ISBN-10: 1512378410

www.ingramcontent.com/pod-product-compliance
Lightning Source LLC
Chambersburg PA
CBHW070818180526
45168CB00002B/667